My Heart Belongs to Jesus (But)

R. J. Carter

Cover design, book design, typesetting by George Peter Gatsis. GeorgePeterGatsis • com

First Edition 2026
0 9 8 7 6 5 4 3 2 1

ISBN: 978-1-967199-36-5

Critical Blast Publishing
624 Sunnyhill Drive, Belleville, IL 62223

CriticalBlast.com / PRINTED IN USA.

Baritone

MY HEART BELONGS TO JESUS, BUT...

said "I play for the Lord But e-ven saints get temp-ted and bored." Then she took my hand

like she al - rea-dy had a plan.__ She said "I won't

fol-low you down that road, And I won't__ car-ry half your load,__ But I__

know how this night__ can__ end."_____ She

set her Bi - ble down nice and neat Said "Faith's__ for keeps but flesh is weak And I won't

ask for gi-veness till the mor-nin comes a - gain."_____ Nei-ther

BRIDGE

one of us were put-tin down roots, She but-toned up while I pulled on my boots. I tipped my

hat. And I gave her a nod.__ She smiled

Baritone

51 Em ... D

soft_ as I left her bed. She's still a vi-sion in-side my_ head. She's still the

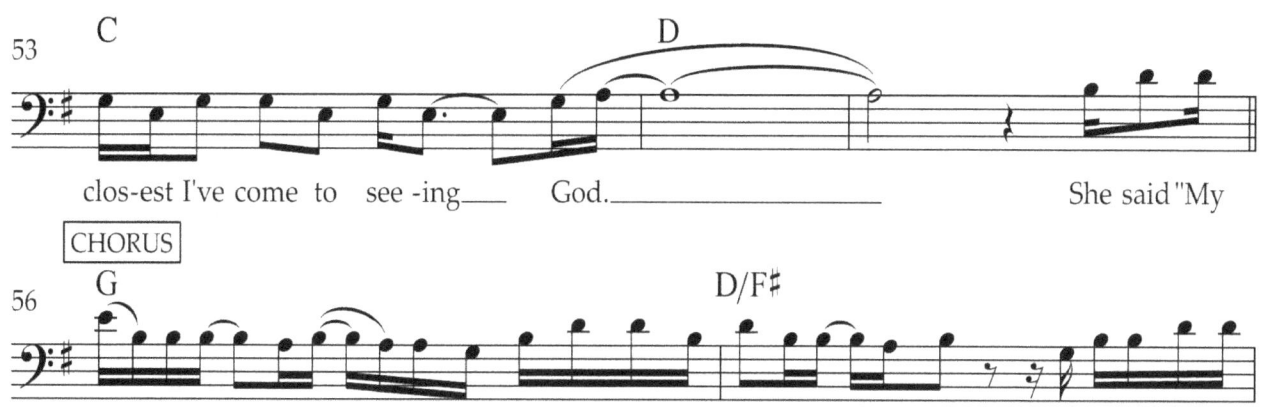

53 C ... D

clos-est I've come to see-ing___ God._____ She said "My

CHORUS

56 G ... D/F♯

heart be-longs to Je - sus, But you can have the rest of me_ to-night. I try to walk a

58 Em ... C

righ-teous path But some times I need to feel earth - ly_ de-lights. I love the way you

60 G ... D/F♯

walk and talk_ But more than once with you__would not_ be right, cause my_

62 Em ... C

heart be-longs__ to Je - sus__ But you can have_ what's left of me_ to-night."

G   Gmaj7/F♯   Em   C   G

64

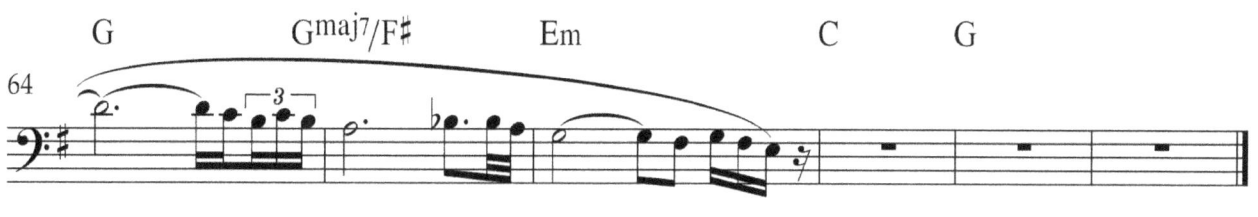

MY HEART BELONGS TO JESUS, BUT...

I rode in - to town

__ with the dust and heat, A lone - some man __ tryin' to make ends meet, When a hymn __ rolled

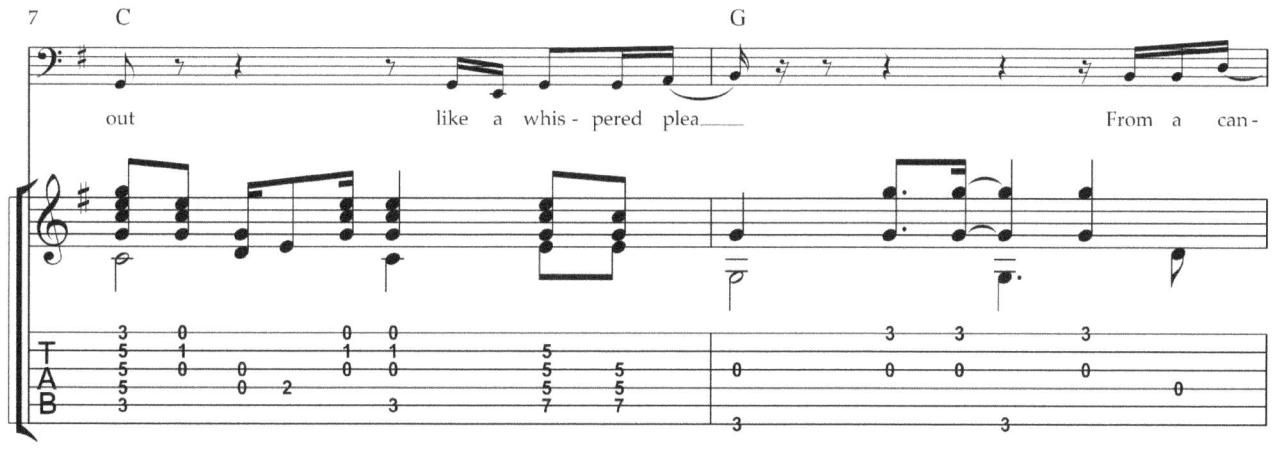

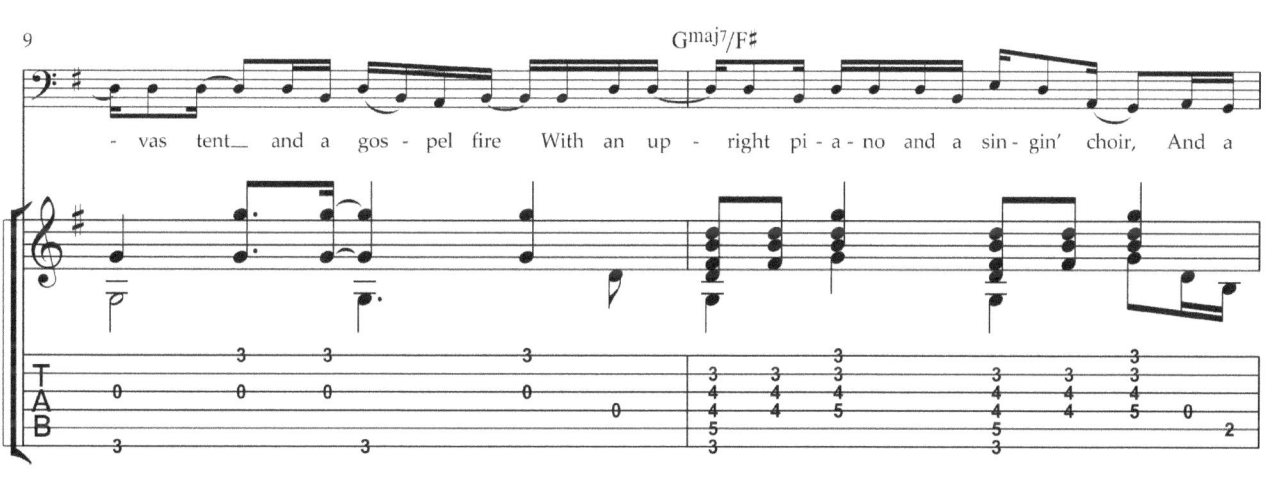

2

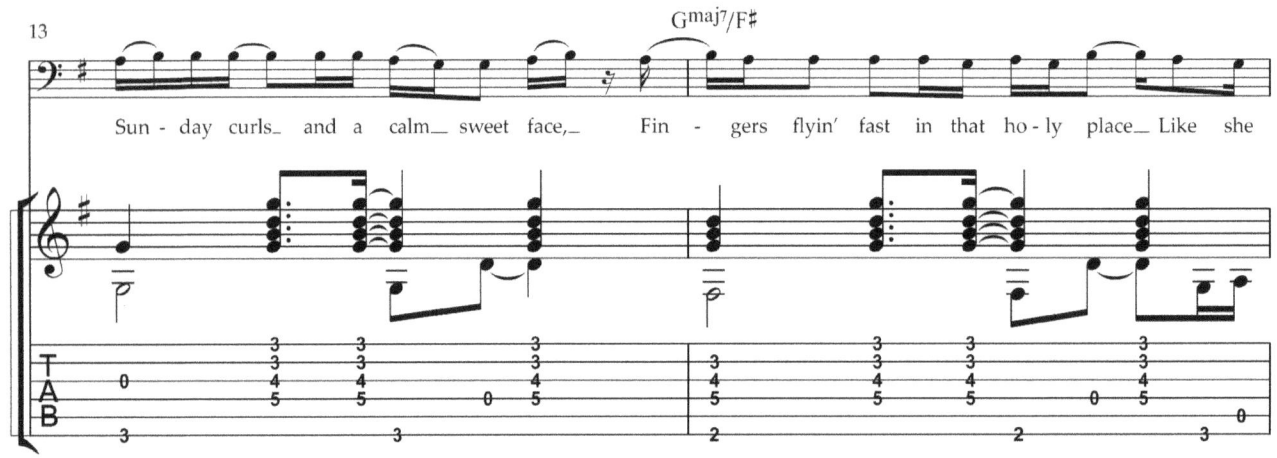

Sun-day curls_ and a calm_ sweet face,_ Fin - gers flyin' fast in that ho - ly place Like she

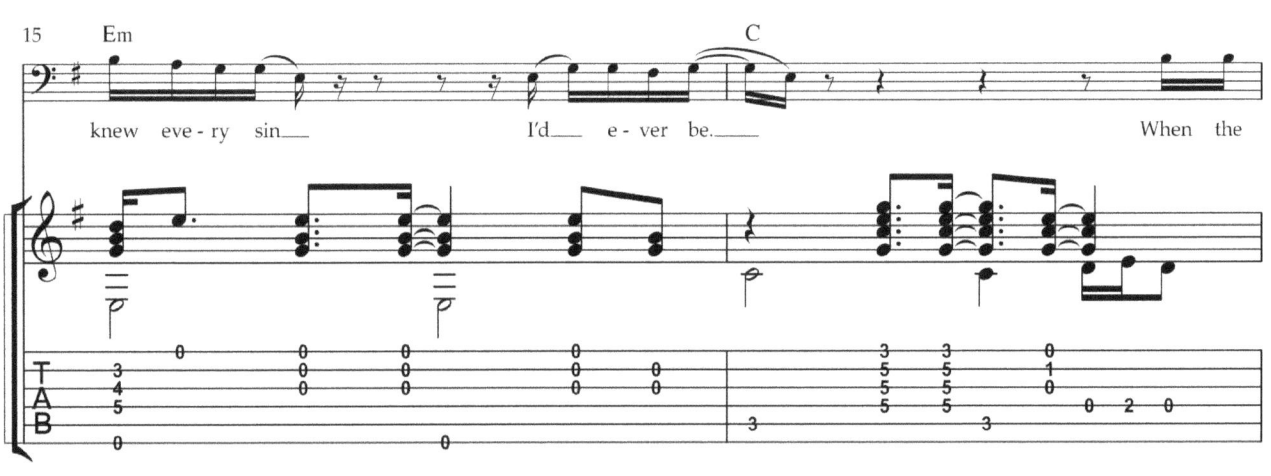

knew eve - ry sin_ I'd e - ver be._ When the

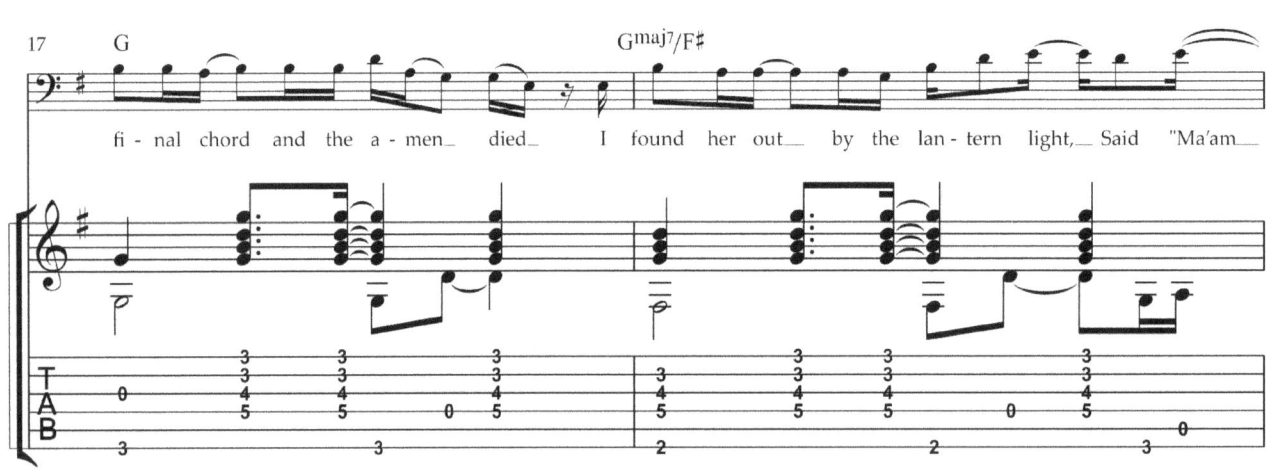

fi - nal chord and the a - men_ died_ I found her out_ by the lan - tern light,_ Said "Ma'am

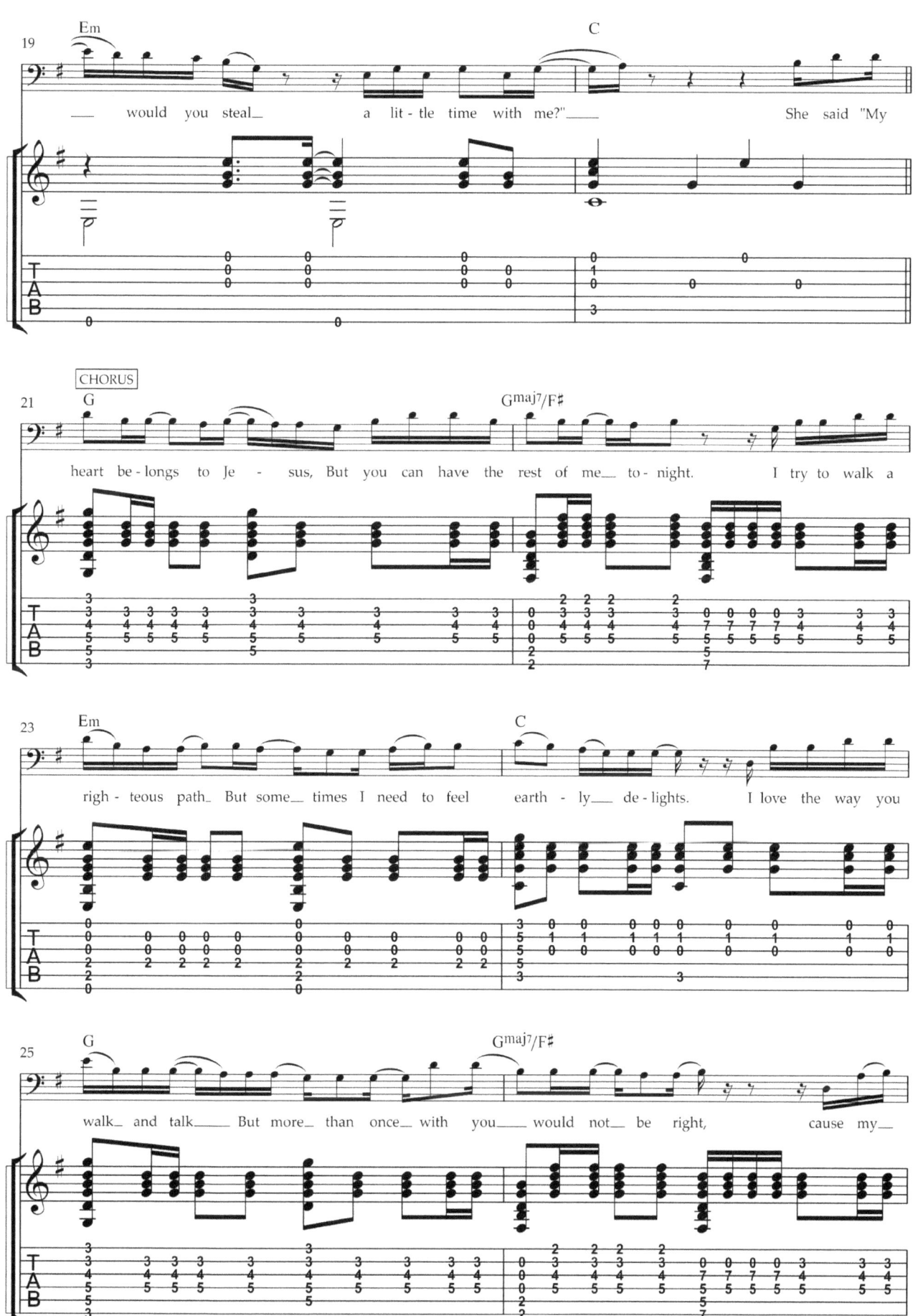

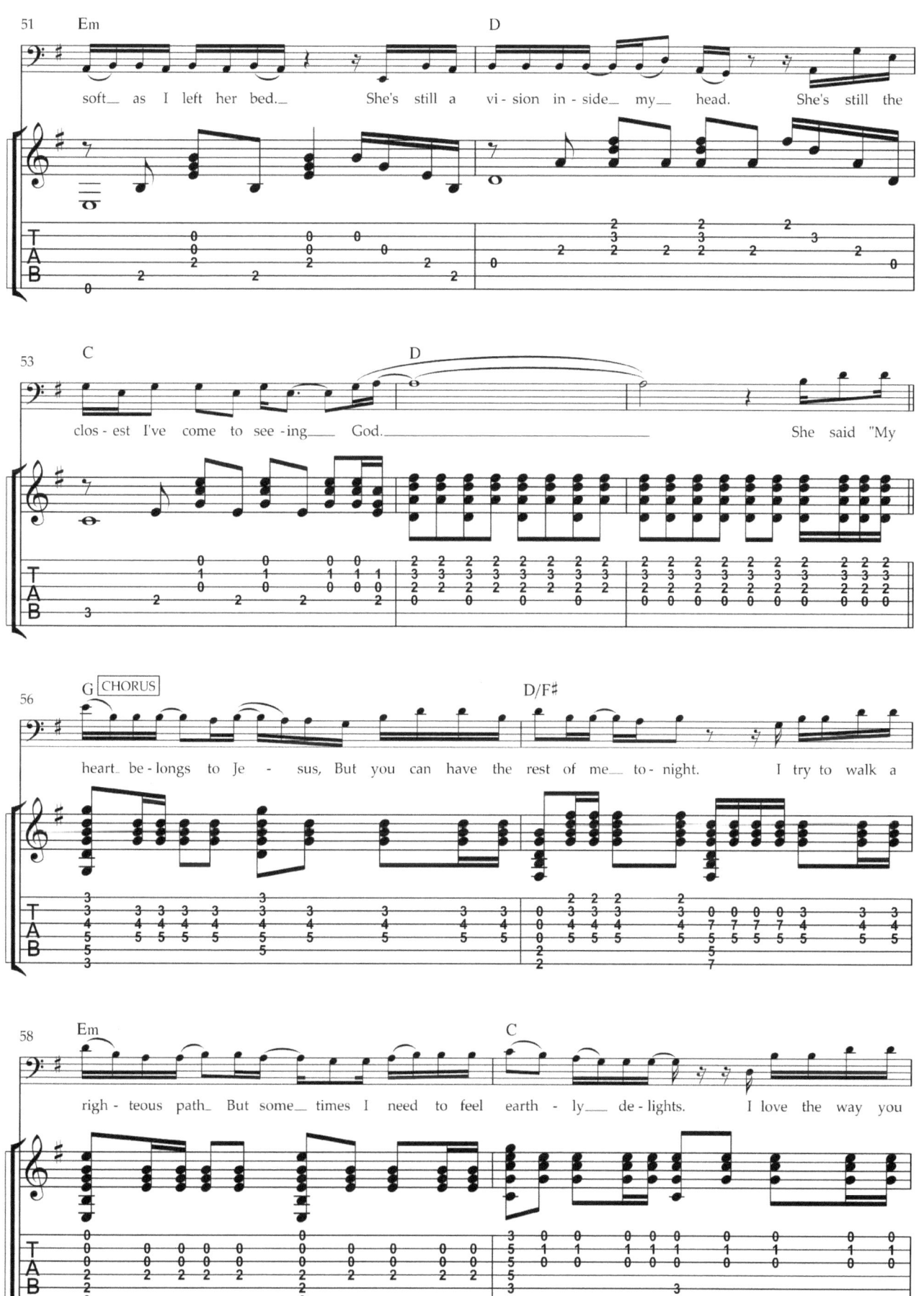

8

www.ingramcontent.com/pod-product-compliance
Lightning Source LLC
Chambersburg PA
CBHW041646120626

46547CB00017B/2625